Original title:
Love's Reflections

Author: Liina Liblikas
ISBN HARDBACK: 978-9916-89-208-4
ISBN PAPERBACK: 978-9916-89-209-1
ISBN EBOOK: 978-9916-89-210-7

A Dance of Ages

In twilight's glow, the shadows sway,
Whispers of time in the soft decay.
Footsteps trace where moments meet,
A rhythm found in the heart's beat.

Beneath the stars, memories twirl,
Echoes of laughter, a gentle whirl.
A tapestry woven in endless grace,
Each thread of joy, our shared embrace.

Seasons shift in a silent dance,
Nature's tune offers each chance.
With open arms, the past extends,
A loving bond that never ends.

In every age, we find our truth,
The dreams of yesterday hold the roots.
In every glance, a story told,
A timeless connection, rich and bold.

So let us sway through night and day,
In this dance, we find our way.
For ages may pass, yet we remain,
In harmony, love's sweet refrain.

Finding Home in You

In the quiet hours, I search and roam,
Through echoes and whispers, I find my home.
With every heartbeat, with every sigh,
You are the beacon that lights the sky.

Your laughter dances with the air,
A melody sweet, beyond compare.
In your embrace, I lose my fears,
A sanctuary built through the years.

The world may shift like sand on shore,
But in your presence, I need no more.
In every glance, the stars align,
A promise kept, forever mine.

As seasons change and rivers flow,
In your arms, my heart will grow.
Your love, a compass, guides me through,
Every journey, I'm home with you.

So here we stand, upon this ground,
In your love, my soul is found.
With every breath, together anew,
In this life, I find my home in you.

The Art of Together

In shared silence, hearts align,
With every glance, our worlds entwine.
Hands interlace, a gentle grace,
Together in this sacred space.

Laughter echoes, soft and bright,
Painting dreams on canvas light.
Steps in sync, we dance as one,
In harmony, our journey's begun.

Moments stitched like threads of gold,
In a tapestry of stories told.
Through storms we stand, through trials we thrive,
In the art of together, we come alive.

When shadows fall, we keep the spark,
Lighting paths within the dark.
With whispered hopes and tender vows,
Love's masterpiece, we craft, allows.

In quietude, we find our song,
A melody that feels so strong.
With each heartbeat, love will tether,
In the beauty of the art: together.

Waves at Twilight

As the sun dips in the sea,
Waves whisper secrets, wild and free.
Colors blend, a canvas bright,
Creating magic in twilight's light.

Footprints fade on sandy shores,
As night embraces, the ocean roars.
Stars awaken, twinkling high,
Reflecting dreams in the darkened sky.

Each ripple tells a tale of days,
Of sunlit smiles and gentle rays.
In silence deep, we stand so near,
As waves embrace each whispered fear.

The moon rises, casting its glow,
Guiding boats through tides that flow.
In this moment, peace we find,
As nature's heartbeat calms the mind.

In the twilight, hearts unite,
With every wave, our spirits light.
In this dance of water's grace,
We find our home, our sacred place.

The Heart's Mosaic

Fragments of love, scattered wide,
In every piece, a story inside.
Colors merge in a vibrant blend,
Creating a path where dreams ascend.

Each shard glimmers with memories bright,
Illuminating shadows, igniting light.
In every crack, a gentle sigh,
The heart's mosaic never lies.

With tender hands, we fit each part,
Building a canvas, a work of art.
Crafted from laughter, stitched with tears,
A masterpiece that conquers fears.

As we piece together our past,
We find a beauty that will last.
In unity's glow, the heart will soar,
A mosaic of love, forevermore.

Through every challenge, we will stand,
With open hearts and joining hands.
In life's gallery, boldly displayed,
The heart's mosaic, never to fade.

Threads of Destiny

In the loom of life, we weave,
Threads of fate that we believe.
Twists and turns in intricate designs,
Unraveling truths where meaning shines.

Each strand connects, a tale unique,
In every knot, the heart will speak.
With patience born from hopes and dreams,
We shape our lives through silent screams.

As seasons change, the colors flow,
In the tapestry of what we know.
Some threads are coarse, while others fine,
Together crafting tales divine.

With gentle hands, we pull so tight,
Creating warmth in the coldest night.
Our destinies intertwined so close,
In this fabric, our love grows.

In every weave, a lesson learned,
With every stitch, a passion burned.
Threads of destiny bind us near,
In life's grand loom, we conquer fear.

The Flow of Forever

Time drifts like a whisper,
Carried by the gentle breeze.
Moments weave through the ether,
Dancing with infinite ease.

Echoes of laughter linger,
In the depths of silent dreams.
Life's a song, a soft singer,
Flowing through untold streams.

Stars twinkle like old stories,
Guiding our hearts through the night.
In their glow, we find glories,
Fleeting yet brilliant and bright.

Tomorrow's promise is waiting,
In the arms of today's light.
Hope is a river, sedating,
Guiding us through every plight.

As the seasons keep turning,
We learn what it means to grow.
In the flow, there's yearning,
For the peace that we sow.

Ripples of Memory

In the pond of reflection,
Ripples spread wide and free.
Each drop holds connection,
A thread of you and me.

Whispers of moments past,
Glimmers in twilight's embrace.
Time slips away so fast,
Yet love leaves a lasting trace.

Fragments of laughter echo,
Like petals on the stream,
In silence, they softly flow,
Weaving through every dream.

The heart bends, but it never breaks,
Each memory a precious stone.
In the fabric of life, it makes,
A tapestry all our own.

Through the waves, memories beckon,
Inviting the heart to mend.
In those ripples, we reckon,
The beginning meets the end.

Lanterns in the Fog

Mist wraps the world in shadows,
Softly draping the ground.
Out of the haze, a glow shows,
A lantern's light can be found.

Guiding the lost through the twilight,
Each flicker tells a tale.
In the stillness of the night,
Hope shines bright, never pale.

With each step, the path reveals,
Secrets hidden from the day.
Lanterns weave a fate that heals,
Lighting our uncertain way.

In the fog, we're not alone,
Connected through light's embrace.
Every glow, a whispered tone,
Carving warmth in silent space.

As the dawn begins to break,
Fog gives way to the sun's grace.
The lanterns, memories we make,
Guide us to a safer place.

A Soul's Collage

Fragments of life stitched together,
A mosaic of joy and pain.
Colors that blend like the weather,
In sunshine or softly falling rain.

Moments like brush strokes on canvas,
Each telling a story of heart.
From laughter and tears, we can grasp,
The beauty of life as an art.

Echoes of dreams and ambitions,
In every piece, a reminder.
Threads of hope and transitions,
Making the soul even kinder.

Whispers of love intertwined,
In shadows and shimmering light.
A collage, uniquely designed,
Reflecting the journey in flight.

As the tapestry unfolds,
We embrace all that we see.
In the soul's collage, behold,
The many shades of being free.

The Silence Between Us

In quiet moments, whispers fade,
A bond unspoken, yet well-made.
Two hearts align in stillness deep,
In the silence, secrets keep.

Stars above in silent gaze,
Guide our hearts through foggy haze.
Between our words, a world we find,
In silence, love is redefined.

Thoughts exchanged without a sound,
In this space, our souls are bound.
The quiet speaks of what we share,
In the stillness, we lay bare.

A gentle touch, a knowing glance,
In the hush, we take a chance.
For in our silence, hearts converse,
In love's embrace, we immerse.

As time unfolds, the silence grows,
Through every joy, each tear that flows.
Together, we find strength in trust,
In the silence, our love is just.

Hearts in Harmony

Two beats converge, a rhythm sweet,
In every laugh, our souls compete.
With every song the world provides,
Together, in this dance, we glide.

A symphony in simple grace,
In every smile, a warm embrace.
The notes of love, we play them true,
In harmony, just me and you.

Fingers intertwined, we sway,
In melody, we find our way.
Beneath the stars, our dreams take flight,
In hearts aligned, we shine so bright.

Through every challenge, every test,
In perfect tune, we find our rest.
With every tear, and every cheer,
In harmony, we conquer fear.

Our song will play through night and day,
In every word, the love we say.
Together bound in sweet refrain,
In hearts in harmony, we gain.

The Dance of Souls

In shadows soft, our spirits twine,
A dance of souls, your hand in mine.
With every step, the world we leave,
In this embrace, we both believe.

A twirl of laughter, freedom found,
In silent motions, depths unbound.
With every sway, the universe swells,
In this rhythm, love compels.

Through light and dark, we spin and sway,
In perfect time, we chase the day.
With whispered dreams, we take our flight,
In the dance of souls, pure delight.

As seasons change, our melody flows,
In every heartbeat, love still grows.
Together we weave the threads of fate,
In this dance, we celebrate.

When music fades, and stillness reigns,
In quiet moments, love remains.
Forever bound, we'll always stay,
In the dance of souls, come what may.

Embracing the Light

In darkest nights, a spark ignites,
A beacon shines, dispelling fights.
With open arms, we seek the bright,
Together, we embrace the light.

Through winding paths and heavy stone,
In shared warmth, we are not alone.
With every step, we find our way,
In love's embrace, we seize the day.

The sun awakes, a gentle glow,
With every heartbeat, we will grow.
In every moment, hope takes flight,
Together, we embrace the light.

Through every storm, our spirits soar,
In union strong, we crave for more.
With laughter bright, we chase the dawn,
In every shadow, we've moved on.

So hand in hand, we walk this path,
With love as guide, and joy as wrath.
Embracing all, both day and night,
Together, we will find the light.

Moonlit Promises

Underneath the silver light,
Whispers dance through the night.
Promises made in shadowed beams,
Wrapped in the fabric of dreams.

Stars above lend their grace,
Guiding hearts in this space.
With each promise softly spoken,
Hearts mend what was once broken.

The moon watches over all,
Casting silver in its call.
In the silence, secrets weave,
Together, we shall believe.

Glimmers of hope in the air,
Moonlit paths for us to share.
Every vow beneath its glow,
With time, our love will grow.

A tapestry of light and fate,
In the night, we celebrate.
Holding tight through the storm,
In moonlit promises, we're warm.

The Ties That Bind

In the echoes of our laugh,
The past whispers its half.
Threads of love, woven tight,
Together, we face the night.

Moments stitched in gold and grace,
A tapestry we embrace.
Through every trial, every tear,
Our bond grows strong and clear.

Distance cannot tear apart,
The ties sewn deep in our heart.
Every challenge, we're aligned,
It's love that truly binds.

Hand in hand, we shall stand,
Facing futures, dreamland.
In every heartbeat, we find,
The strength in ties that bind.

Through the storms and through the light,
Together, we will ignite.
The power of love defined,
Forever, the ties that bind.

Serendipity's Glow

In a twist of fate we find,
Magic lingers, sweetly kind.
Orbits cross in splendid sway,
Serendipity leads the way.

Moments met like sun and breeze,
Creating memories with ease.
When our paths intertwined,
A spark of joy unconfined.

Each turn unexpected, bright,
Guiding hearts to pure delight.
In laughter's echo, we grow,
Bathed in serendipity's glow.

Together, we dance in chance,
Life's unpredictable romance.
With every step, we discover,
In sweet surprises, we uncover.

A journey, wild and free,
With you, it's where I long to be.
In every twist, there's a show,
Of love in serendipity's glow.

A Tapestry of Us

Threads of laughter, joy, and tears,
Woven tight through all our years.
Each moment a colorful thread,
In the tapestry we tread.

Patterns shift and colors blend,
In this art, we choose to mend.
Every story, every sigh,
A piece of us that won't die.

Among the patterns, love will grow,
In every twist, a vibrant glow.
Our hands together, side by side,
Creating a warmth where we confide.

Every chapter, every line,
We build a world that's truly divine.
In love's embrace, trust and rust,
Forever we'll be a tapestry of us.

As time weaves its gentle lace,
We'll find our rhythm, our own pace.
An artwork that never fades,
A tapestry where love cascades.

When Time Stops

In a world where whispers fade,
Silent moments start to wade.
The clock's hands freeze in their flight,
Echoing the still of night.

Dreams unfold in gentle sighs,
Captured under starry skies.
When each heartbeat feels so slow,
Time is lost, yet we still flow.

Memories linger, soft and bright,
Carried by the moon's soft light.
An instant turns to endless frame,
In this pause, we're all the same.

Fleeting shadows dance with grace,
In this timeless, sacred space.
Here, we find what means the most,
Tender love, a quiet toast.

When the world stands still, it's true,
Every moment speaks of you.
Together in the starlit glow,
In this stillness, feelings grow.

The Pulse of Our Journey

With every step we take today,
Our hearts beat strong, come what may.
Through valleys low and mountains high,
Together, we reach for the sky.

With laughter shared and sorrows too,
Each twist and turn brings me to you.
In the dance of fate and chance,
Our spirits rise, they find their stance.

The road is long, the path unclear,
Yet hand in hand, we quell the fear.
Every bend holds a new surprise,
As we chase sunsets, look to the skies.

The stories written on our hands,
Are written in the grains of sands.
With every pulse, we write our song,
In harmony, we all belong.

So let us roam, let us be free,
For life's a quest, just you and me.
In this journey, side by side,
In truth and love, we shall abide.

Echoes of Us

In echoes soft, your voice remains,
A melody that flows like rains.
Each word a whisper in the night,
A treasure lost yet shining bright.

In shadows cast by memories,
Your laughter dances in the breeze.
Through time's embrace, we find our place,
In each reflection, a sweet grace.

The past unfolds with every wave,
An endless tale, both bound and brave.
In every heartbeat, I feel you near,
A symphony that draws us here.

With every glance, the world ignites,
We share the warmth of starlit nights.
The echoes linger, never fade,
In timeless circles, love is made.

Together still, let voices blend,
In this rhythm, we transcend.
For in the echoes of our trust,
We find forever, just for us.

Through Twilit Windows

As twilight paints the sky with gold,
Soft shadows stretch, the day grows old.
Through window panes, the world unwinds,
Glimmers of magic, peace it finds.

Silent whispers dance on air,
Moonlit dreams beyond compare.
In gentle hues, the dusk reveals,
The truth that every heart conceals.

Within these walls, our secrets stay,
Each glance of love won't drift away.
Through twilit windows, we confide,
In every moment, side by side.

With tender warmth, the night unfolds,
As stories of our hearts are told.
Casting spells of hope and grace,
In twilight's arms, we find our place.

Together now, the light grows dim,
Yet in the dark, our hopes don't swim.
Through twilit windows, love will shine,
A beacon bright, forever mine.

In the Embrace of Time

In quiet whispers, moments flow,
Time's gentle touch, an ebb and glow.
Memories dance upon the night,
Fleeting shadows, fading light.

Each tick a story, a breath, a sigh,
Glimmers of joy that never die.
We gather fragments, hold them dear,
In the embrace of time, we're near.

Seasons change, like tides they turn,
Lessons linger, with each we learn.
In the stillness, a heartbeat chimes,
Echoing love through endless climbs.

Grains of sand slip through our hands,
Yet in our souls, forever stands.
A tapestry woven with threads of fate,
In the embrace of time, we wait.

As twilight falls, we share a glance,
Life's fleeting rhythm, a sacred dance.
Together we weave through days so bright,
In the embrace of time, pure light.

A Journey in Bloom

Petals open in morning's grace,
Nature's beauty in every space.
A journey unfolds with each new dawn,
In colors bright, new dreams are drawn.

Each step a story, each leaf a sign,
With roots in the soil, our hearts entwine.
Through valleys wide and mountains high,
We seek the sun, reaching for the sky.

Whispers of wind guide us along,
The rhythm of life, a timeless song.
In laughter shared and tears we weep,
A journey in bloom, our memories keep.

With every storm, we learn to bend,
Resilient spirits, on paths we ascend.
In harmony with the world around,
A journey in bloom, where love is found.

So let us wander, hand in hand,
Creating memories like grains of sand.
In the tapestry of days gone by,
A journey in bloom, we'll never say goodbye.

Shimmering Echoes

In twilight's glow, a soft refrain,
Whispers of dreams that linger, remain.
Shimmering echoes dance in the air,
Fleeting moments, fragile and rare.

Each note a heartbeat, a story untold,
Woven in light, as memories unfold.
In silken shadows, we find our way,
Shimmering echoes of yesterday.

Through the silence, a melody swells,
A tapestry woven with wishes and spells.
In the stillness, our spirits take flight,
Shimmering echoes that shine through the night.

Finding solace in paths we roam,
A symphony played in rhythms of home.
Longing and laughter weave through the air,
Shimmering echoes, a breath of prayer.

As starlight fades and dawn draws near,
We gather our dreams, all that we hold dear.
In the brightness of futures we see,
Shimmering echoes, you and me.

The Path of Us

Two souls entwined on life's great road,
Together we carry a shared strong load.
With every step, the world unfolds,
The path of us, as time beholds.

Through fields of gold and skies of blue,
In every heartbeat, our love rings true.
Hand in hand, we'll brave the night,
Guided by stars that shine so bright.

Challenges rise, like mountains steep,
Yet in our bond, our faith runs deep.
With laughter and tears, we face each test,
Along the path of us, we are blessed.

Whispers of dreams in the morning light,
Together we weave through day and night.
In the journey ahead, our spirits soar,
The path of us, forevermore.

As seasons change and moments flow,
In the heart's embrace, our love will grow.
With every heartbeat, our story thus,
We walk this life, the path of us.

Shards of Togetherness

In the light of morning glow,
We gather pieces, soft and slow.
With laughter ringing, hearts unite,
Shards of moments, pure and bright.

Through whispered dreams, our souls entwine,
In every story, you're a sign.
Held together amidst the storm,
In unity, our spirits warm.

Echoes linger in the air,
A tapestry of love laid bare.
With every breath, we weave and spin,
In these shards, our journey begins.

Though time may challenge, we won't break,
In every step, the bonds we make.
Fueled by hope, we rise anew,
Together's where our hearts break through.

Fragmented yet so beautifully whole,
In each other, we find our role.
Through whispered dreams and laughter shared,
In these shards, our love declared.

Glimmers of Devotion

Underneath the starry skies,
We find the truth behind our eyes.
With every glance, a promise blooms,
In glimmers bright, devotion looms.

In quiet moments, hands embrace,
Time stands still in this sacred space.
With tender whispers, we ignite,
Each glimmer shines, a beacon bright.

Through trials faced and laughter high,
Our spirits dance like flames that fly.
Each flicker strong, through night and day,
In every heartbeat, love's array.

In memories shared, we chalk our dreams,
Glimmers of hope in moonlit beams.
Together forged in fires strong,
In this devotion, we belong.

With radiant joy, our hearts take flight,
In glimmers' glow, we find our light.
Forever bound in love's embrace,
In every moment, we find grace.

Shadows of Intimacy

In the soft, dim light of dusk,
Our secrets shared, a sacred trust.
In every hush, our voices blend,
Shadows twine as lovers mend.

In whispered dreams, we softly tread,
With ethereal words, our hearts are fed.
Each stolen glance beneath the moon,
In shadows cast, our spirits swoon.

Through tangled memories, we explore,
Each shadow holds a hidden door.
In silence shared, a bond so deep,
In intimacy, love we keep.

As night embraces our careful sighs,
We lose ourselves in boundless skies.
With every touch, the world fades away,
In shadows' grace, we wish to stay.

In the echoes of our quiet nights,
We find the spark that ignites.
In whispered tones and tender hands,
Shadows dance where love understands.

Petals in the Stream

Drifting gently on the flow,
Petals whisper tales we know.
Carried softly by the breeze,
In the stream, our hearts find ease.

As blossoms fall, we let them glide,
In nature's current, love's sweet ride.
With every ripple, memories gleam,
Our life unfolds, a cherished theme.

Through seasons shifting, petals sway,
In joyful laughter, come what may.
Together floating, side by side,
In the stream, our dreams abide.

With every moment, layers shed,
In the journey, we will tread.
With petals bright, our wishes streamed,
In life's flow, we've always dreamed.

As twilight casts its gentle hue,
We send our hopes where dreams come true.
Like petals dancing, pure and free,
In the stream, just you and me.

The Language of Gazes

In the silence, eyes meet light,
Whispers dance in the twilight.
Stories told without a word,
A symphony, unobserved.

Shadows linger, hearts entwine,
In that glance, our souls align.
Unspoken tales in every stare,
A gentle pull, a tender snare.

Moments freeze, time stands still,
In their depths, a silent thrill.
Words may fail, yet truth remains,
Emotion flows through unseen veins.

Behind closed lids, visions flare,
Hopes take flight in the air.
Sparks ignite with a slight tilt,
A world built on the gaze we built.

Through the veil, a longing sigh,
Dreams reflect as hearts fly high.
In the tender dance of light,
The language of gazes ignites.

Ink and Stardust

Across white pages, dreams take flight,
Ink flows freely, hearts ignite.
Words like constellations bloom,
Crafting worlds that banish gloom.

With every stroke, magic spills,
Stardust dances, the cosmos thrill.
Stories woven with care and heart,
From universe to world, a work of art.

The pen, a wand, creates a spark,
Illuminating corners dark.
A tapestry of thoughts expressed,
In ink and stardust, we are blessed.

Each letter formed a universe vast,
Echoes of futures, shadows of past.
With whispered secrets, lives unfurl,
In the magic of ink, we form our world.

As pages turn, new realms arise,
Adventures written beneath the skies.
In starlit dreams, we find our way,
Ink and stardust, in endless play.

Chasing Sunsets

Golden hues paint the evening sky,
As day fades softly, sighs comply.
Footsteps echo on sandy shores,
Chasing daylight as twilight pours.

The horizon blurs with shades of fire,
Every moment fuels desire.
Whispers of dusk beckon us near,
In the warmth of yellowing cheer.

We run where colors intertwine,
Hearts racing like a vintage wine.
In every sunset, dreams collide,
Chasing shadows, with time our guide.

Silhouettes dance against the glow,
Memory's tide begins to flow.
Each setting sun a promise made,
In the canvas of night, we wade.

With every sunset, stories are spun,
A fleeting moment, dusk's last run.
In pursuit of beauty, we find our way,
Chasing sunsets, night to day.

Reflections in Raindrops

Each raindrop holds a world inside,
Mirrors of dreams, where hopes abide.
Shimmering on leaves, a dance of light,
In their embrace, the day feels bright.

Puddles form like portals old,
Secrets of the earth, stories told.
With every drop, a tale unfolds,
Wonders of life in reflections bold.

In stormy skies, our fears are shed,
Raindrops fall, echoing what's said.
Nature's tears, both joy and woe,
In the chorus of rain, feelings flow.

Through windows, droplets race and glide,
Life's fleeting moments, a joyous ride.
Chasing shadows, we lose and find,
Reflections in raindrops, hearts entwined.

As storms recede, the world feels new,
Colors awakened, a vibrant hue.
In every droplet, connections align,
Reflections in raindrops, love's design.

Ripples of Devotion

In the stillness of night,
Whispers dance on the water.
Each heartbeat a promise,
Embracing love's soft laughter.

Through the storms that may rise,
Together we'll face the tide.
With every sigh, our bond
Grows stronger, side by side.

In shadows cast by the moon,
We find solace in silence.
Every moment together,
A shared sweet, sweet reliance.

With every step we take,
Ripples grow wide and far.
Echoes of our devotion,
Guided by our love star.

As dawn breaks the dark veil,
Hope flickers like the sun.
In this journey of hearts,
Together, we are one.

Silhouettes of Passion

In twilight's warm embrace,
Shadows merge, hearts ignite.
With every stolen glance,
Our souls take flight at night.

Soft whispers cross the dark,
Promises linger and swirl.
In the dance of soft sighs,
Our love begins to unfurl.

Underneath the bright stars,
We share secrets, we dare.
Two silhouettes entwined,
In a world, just we share.

Each heartbeat syncs with time,
As we paint the night bold.
With tender brushstrokes, love,
Crafting tales yet untold.

When day breaks, we'll still hold,
The fire we felt, the glow.
In the morning light, we'll rise,
Together, hearth and soul.

Journey of Two Hearts

We set sail on this road,
Carried by dreams untold.
With every stride we take,
Our story starts to unfold.

Through valleys deep and wide,
Together, hand in hand.
With each laugh, each tear shed,
A brighter future, we planned.

Mountains may tower high,
Yet love will guide us true.
In every climb we face,
I'll always turn to you.

Underneath the night sky,
Stars light our winding path.
Together, hearts united,
In joy and in our wrath.

As seasons change and flow,
Through time, we'll weave our thread.
In this journey of hearts,
By love, we shall be led.

A Palette of Desires

With colors bright and bold,
We paint our dreams each day.
In strokes of joy and hope,
Love guides us on our way.

Each hue tells a story,
Of laughter and of tears.
A canvas filled with passion,
Overcoming all our fears.

With every brush we wield,
Desires come to life.
In shades of deep affection,
We banish pain and strife.

The masterpiece of us,
Unfolding, ever grand.
A palette of our hearts,
Together, we will stand.

As sunset paints the sky,
With hues of love's delight.
In this art of living,
We bask in colors bright.

Stargazing Hearts

Under the vast and endless night,
We trace the stars with hearts alight.
Each twinkle tells of dreams untold,
In whispers soft, our wishes fold.

In silent awe, we stand and gaze,
Lost in the cosmos' gentle blaze.
Connecting souls in silence shared,
Together, lost, yet unprepared.

With each constellation that we find,
Our hearts entwined as souls aligned.
The universe, it sings our song,
In harmony, we both belong.

The moon above, a watchful friend,
Guides our journey without end.
In starlit skies, we find our way,
Each heartbeat draws us more to stay.

As dawn arrives, the stars do fade,
Yet in our hearts, their light cascades.
With stargazing hearts, we will remain,
In memories bright, we feel no pain.

Elysium of Affection

In a realm where love does bloom,
Soft whispers melt away the gloom.
Each glance exchanged, a spark ignites,
In the Elysium, pure delights.

Through fields of gold, we wander free,
Hand in hand, just you and me.
The air is sweet with every sigh,
In this haven, love will fly.

With every step, our laughter rings,
Like gentle songs that joy can bring.
Our hearts entwined, a dance divine,
In this paradise, your heart is mine.

Beneath the boughs of ancient trees,
We find our pace, our perfect breeze.
In every moment shared, we weave,
A tapestry of love, believe.

As stars emerge in twilight's grace,
We chase the night, our sacred space.
In Elysium, our souls take flight,
Basking in affection's light.

Lanterns in the Fog

In the mist, we walk as one,
Soft lanterns glow, our journey begun.
Each flicker holds a tale so bright,
Guiding us through the shrouded night.

Whispers of secrets in the air,
A gentle breeze stirs dreams to share.
With every step, the fog reveals,
What love can be, what heart conceals.

The lanterns sway with every breath,
Lighting paths that defy the depths.
In the dance of shadows and light,
We find our way, igniting night.

With hope aglow, we chase the dawn,
In foggy realms, where love is drawn.
Together we face the unknown, bold,
Our hearts a blaze, our stories told.

As morning breaks, the mist will part,
But lanterns linger in each heart.
Through journeys vast, we learned to trust,
In the fog, it's love, it's us.

Petals of Affection

On gentle winds, your laughter plays,
Like petals dancing in sunlit rays.
Soft whispers circle, sweet and bright,
In every moment, pure delight.

We wander through a blooming field,
In nature's arms, our love revealed.
Each petal serves a silent vow,
Our hearts are blooming, here and now.

With colors bold, our love displayed,
In every hue, sweet memories made.
Fall into this embrace divine,
With petals soft, our souls entwine.

Through seasons change, our bond will grow,
As flowers bloom and rivers flow.
With every petal that we share,
We weave a love beyond compare.

As twilight falls, the petals rest,
In gentle folds, our hearts are blessed.
In every heartbeat, we will find,
Petals of affection, forever twined.

Sketches on the Canvas

Colors dance with gentle grace,
Each stroke an embrace.
Whispers of dreams take flight,
In the soft morning light.

Textures blend in harmony,
A story waits to be free.
Lines converge and expand,
A vision, carefully planned.

In shadows, secrets lie,
Awaiting the artist's sigh.
Each hue tells a tale,
In this colorful gale.

A heartbeat flows through space,
Beauty found in every trace.
Storylines intertwine,
Creating a world divine.

Brush in hand, heart in tow,
As the artistry begins to grow.
From chaos emerges peace,
In a masterpiece's release.

Murmurs of the Night

Stars twinkle in the vastness above,
Echoes of the moon's soft love.
Whispers weave through the trees,
Carried lightly by the breeze.

Shadows dance in twilight's realm,
While dreams begin to overwhelm.
Candles flicker, casting light,
Guiding us through the night.

Silence sings a soothing tune,
Crickets chirp beneath the moon.
Mysteries shroud the dark sky,
As the nightbirds softly cry.

Each moment holds a secret sigh,
As time holds still, we learn to fly.
In the stillness, souls connect,
In dreams, we find respect.

The night, a canvas of our fears,
Woven with laughter and tears.
Here in shadows, hope glows bright,
In the sweet murmurs of the night.

A Universe Between Us

In the quiet spaces we share,
Countless stars spark in the air.
Galaxies collide in our gaze,
Infinite connections amaze.

Words linger like celestial light,
Guiding souls through the night.
In this vast, cosmic dance,
A single glance, a chance.

Time stretches like a longing sigh,
Across the sky, love won't die.
Each heartbeat travels far,
A wish upon a distant star.

The universe holds us tight,
With every breath, we ignite.
In the silence, we both see,
A vast eternity.

Souls entwined, worlds collide,
In the beauty of love's tide.
Together, we weave our fate,
In this universe, it's never too late.

The Ties of Tomorrow

Threads of dreams softly spun,
Binding hearts as we run.
Futures whispered in the dusk,
Building hope, a steadfast trust.

With every step, we forge a path,
Navigating the aftermath.
Laughter dances in the air,
As we chase what we dare.

The tapestry of days ahead,
Each moment, a word unsaid.
In the fabric of our lives,
Together, love survives.

Challenges rise like mountains tall,
But hand in hand, we shall not fall.
In the bonds that weave and twine,
A bright future will shine.

Through trials, we shall grow strong,
Together is where we belong.
The ties of tomorrow unfold,
In stories waiting to be told.

Secrets in Silence

In whispers soft, the night unfolds,
Hidden tales that the stillness holds.
Moonlight dances on quiet streams,
Eclipsing thoughts, revealing dreams.

Shadows waltz with gentle grace,
Time stands still in this sacred space.
Each breath lingers, a fleeting sigh,
Moments captured as echoes fly.

Silence speaks in the heart's refrain,
A symphony of joy and pain.
Between the notes, the secrets hide,
A journey taken, side by side.

Listen close, the stillness calls,
In silence where the spirit falls.
From depths unknown, a truth is born,
In the quiet, a new dawn's worn.

So let us wander, hearts in tune,
In the hush beneath the moon.
For in each silence, love takes flight,
Whispered secrets of the night.

Resonance of Dreams

In twilight's haze, the visions wake,
Echoes soft, like ripples make.
The heart beats with a hopeful sound,
In every dream, new paths are found.

Stars align in the canvas sky,
Painting futures where spirits fly.
Awake to wonder, let thoughts soar,
Each dream a wave upon the shore.

Gentle whispers of longing hearts,
In the realm where the magic starts.
Every heartbeat casts a spell,
In this resonance, we dwell.

The night air hums with melodies,
As shadows dance in the evening breeze.
Embrace the silence, let it gleam,
For life's a dance, and love's the theme.

So chase the dawn with open eyes,
In every moment, let hope rise.
For in the dreams, the world awakes,
In the warmth of love, our spirit breaks.

Ephemeral Embrace

Fleeting moments like grains of sand,
Slipping softly through gentle hands.
Each breath a whisper, a kiss of time,
In the fleeting, love's rhythm chimes.

Sunset's glow paints the evening sky,
A tapestry woven, we say goodbye.
In the twilight, we find our grace,
In tender moments, an endless chase.

Every heartbeat tells its tale,
A journey written on love's frail sail.
A touch that lingers, a gaze that stays,
In the ephemeral, our spirit plays.

Seasons change, but memories stay,
Echoing softly, like a song's sway.
In every parting, a bond remains,
In the ephemeral, love gains.

So let us cherish, each moment's glow,
For through the fleeting, our true hearts grow.
In this embrace, we learn to see,
The beauty found in eternity.

Threads of Connection

In a world of light, shadows intertwine,
Each soul a thread, a pattern divine.
Through laughter and tears, the fabric we weave,
In every encounter, we learn to believe.

Tiny moments, like stitches, align,
Creating a tapestry, yours and mine.
With every story, a bond we find,
A network of hearts, tenderly twined.

Distance may stretch, but connections hold,
A warmth in the silence, a comfort bold.
Through whispered dreams and shared delight,
We find each other in the night.

As seasons change, we may drift apart,
But the threads remain, joined by the heart.
In every glance, a memory bright,
In every heartbeat, a shared flight.

So honor the ties that fate has spun,
In every journey, we are one.
For in connections, life finds its song,
In the threads of love, we all belong.

Luminous Connections

In the twilight, we find our place,
Soft whispers linger, memories trace.
Stars unite, a cosmic flare,
Hearts collide in the evening air.

Threads of light bind us tight,
Woven stories in the night.
Every glance, a spark ignites,
Together, we dance in endless flights.

Echoes of laughter fill the sky,
Timeless bonds that never die.
In silence, we share our dreams,
Boundless hope in moonlit beams.

Through vast oceans, our souls roam,
Each distant star, a guiding home.
In the glow of cherished days,
We find love in countless ways.

As the dawn begins to rise,
With golden hues, our spirits fly.
For in this life, we are defined,
By luminous connections intertwined.

Heartstrings Entwined

In the melody of softest sighs,
We discover where true love lies.
A symphony played, hearts align,
Two souls dancing, a love divine.

Through trials faced, we grow strong,
In the chorus where we belong.
Echoes of sweetness, words unspoken,
Promises shared, never broken.

With every heartbeat, a gentle thread,
Nestled close, where dreams are fed.
The rhythm of us flows like a stream,
Entwined together, we weave our dream.

In moments fleeting, joy we seek,
Silent vows in whispers peak.
With hands held tight, we shall endure,
In the dance of hearts, love is pure.

As twilight unfolds its tender hue,
In twilight's promise, I find you.
An everlasting bond we'll define,
With heartstrings forever entwined.

Through Your Eyes

In your gaze, the world ignites,
Colors bloom in soft delights.
A universe in shades of gold,
Every secret, tenderly told.

Reflections dance in pools so deep,
Where dreams wade, and shadows leap.
Through your eyes, I see the sun,
The beauty in life, we've just begun.

With every blink, a story spins,
Glances share where love begins.
A tapestry of memories bright,
Woven closely, day meets night.

In your vision, time stands still,
Moments cherished, hearts to fill.
Through your eyes, the stars converge,
A love song where we both emerge.

So let us wander, hand in hand,
Through the landscapes, together we stand.
For in your eyes, I find my way,
Guided by love, come what may.

A Dance of Souls

In twilight's embrace, we take our stance,
Two hearts flutter, caught in a chance.
With every step, a rhythm so fine,
A dance of souls, a love divine.

The music swells, the night unfolds,
In whispered secrets, stories told.
With grace we twirl, the world fades away,
In this moment, where we wish to stay.

As shadows join in our gentle sway,
We celebrate life in the softest way.
Each spin a promise, each leap a sigh,
In this dance of souls, we learn to fly.

The stars above watch our embrace,
Two kindred spirits, time cannot erase.
With every heartbeat, the tempo grows,
In the dance of love, forever flows.

So let our journey continue to weave,
In this tapestry of dreams we believe.
With every step, our stories unfold,
In a dance of souls, forever bold.

Mosaic of Emotions

In colors bright, we find our way,
A canvas filled with shades of gray,
Each brushstroke tells a silent tale,
Of love and loss, we set our sail.

Fragments broken, piece by piece,
In chaos, we seek our release,
Every hue, a moment's grace,
In this mosaic, we find our place.

The laughter echoes, the tears fall down,
In every corner, joy and frown,
Emotions dance, a fragile art,
Together woven, never apart.

A whisper soft, a thunder loud,
In every heartbeat, we are proud,
A symphony of feelings bright,
In every shadow, there's a light.

So here we stand, both cracked and whole,
Each piece a story, each piece a soul,
Embracing all, the storm and sun,
In this mosaic, we are one.

Fragments of Us

Scattered pieces upon the floor,
Memories linger, wanting more,
In every shard, a story stays,
Of laughter lost in brighter days.

Holding tight to what remains,
In every joy, in all the pains,
These fragments weave a tapestry,
A portrait of our mystery.

Time may fade, but love endures,
In every crack, a heart assures,
We gather pieces, hand in hand,
Rebuilding what we understand.

Together strong, we search and find,
Each missing piece refreshes mind,
Our journey told in every mark,
In fragments bright, we light the dark.

So let us cherish every part,
The broken bonds that shape the heart,
As fragments join, a whole anew,
In every piece, I find the you.

The Mirror of Togetherness

In the mirror, we see our face,
Reflections dancing, time and space,
Together bound in every glance,
A silent promise, a shared dance.

Every laugh, a ripple wide,
In this mirror, where we confide,
Hand in hand, we face the light,
In shadows cast, we hold on tight.

Through trials faced, both fierce and bright,
Our unity becomes the light,
In every flaw, a beauty found,
In this mirror, love is crowned.

Every heartbeat whispers true,
In togetherness, we are glue,
In loving glances, we ignite,
The warmth of souls, a guiding light.

So let us stand, side by side,
In the mirror, our hearts confide,
With every truth that we embrace,
In togetherness, we find our place.

Tides of Longing

The ocean whispers secrets low,
Waves of yearning gently flow,
Through restless shores, our hearts are tossed,
In tides of longing, we feel lost.

Each crest holds dreams we wish to share,
In moonlit nights, we find our care,
But every ebb, it pulls away,
Leaving us in a silent gray.

Yet still we wait for the return,
In waves of hope, our spirits burn,
Every crash, a promise made,
In tides of longing, love won't fade.

As stars align, and night grows deep,
In waters dark, our wishes seep,
The currents guide, and hearts will sway,
In tides of longing, we will stay.

So here we stand, with arms outstretched,
In every wave, our souls are etched,
Through every tide, we rise and fall,
In longing's grasp, we feel it all.

The Secrets We Share

In whispered tones we often meet,
A bond that time cannot defeat.
With every glance, a silent vow,
The secrets held between us now.

Through laughter soft and quiet tears,
We kindle trust throughout the years.
Each hidden truth a precious part,
An echo deep within the heart.

In shadows where some fears reside,
We find the strength to turn the tide.
With each confession, lines are drawn,
A map of love, a secret dawn.

In fleeting moments, we confide,
With open arms, we choose to hide.
The stories shared in soft embrace,
Are footprints left in time and space.

Through whispered dreams and quiet nights,
We forge our path in shared delights.
With each new dawn, our spirits soar,
In secrets shared, we're evermore.

A Symphony of Touch

In gentle strokes, we weave a song,
With tender hands where we belong.
Each brush of skin, a note we play,
In perfect harmony, we sway.

A dance of fingers in the night,
In every pulse, a spark ignites.
The rhythm builds with every sigh,
As heartbeats blend, we touch the sky.

In quiet moments, silence speaks,
With every glance, our spirit seeks.
A symphony of soft delight,
Resonates beneath the moonlight.

Through every brush, we tell our tale,
A melody where love prevails.
In every caress, we intertwine,
A sweet embrace, a love divine.

In gentle warmth, our souls align,
Two bodies merge, your heart is mine.
With every touch, the world we claim,
In this symphony, we are the same.

Beneath the Surface

In quiet depths, our secrets lie,
Beneath the waves, where whispers sigh.
The stillness holds what eyes can't see,
A vast expanse of mystery.

The current pulls, the shadows dance,
In every glance, a fleeting chance.
With every tide, our fears subside,
And in the dark, our hearts confide.

In ripples soft, the truth takes flight,
Guiding us through the velvet night.
We dive into the unseen dreams,
Where hope and fear can flow like streams.

A hidden world, a sacred space,
Where love unfolds with gentle grace.
Beneath the surface, we persist,
In every pulse, an unseen twist.

And though the storm may roar and crash,
We'll find the calm in every splash.
In depths so dark, we learn to see,
The beauty held in mystery.

Moments in Stillness

In quietude, we find our truth,
A world unspooled, a cherished youth.
With every breath, the silence speaks,
In moments still, our spirit peaks.

Through tranquil nights and golden dawns,
In precious time, our dream lives on.
With every heartbeat, we reflect,
On love that time cannot neglect.

The world outside may rush and spin,
But in our hearts, we drift within.
A stillness found, a sacred space,
In every pause, we find our grace.

With eyes closed tight, we journey far,
In silent thoughts, we see the stars.
Each moment still, a gem pristine,
In peaceful light, our souls convene.

And as the echoes softly fade,
In stillness' arms, we all have stayed.
With every glance, the world feels new,
In moments still, I dwell with you.

Dancing on Air

Light as a feather, we sway and spin,
Joy in each movement, a whirlwind begins.
Under the moonlight, our laughter takes flight,
Two souls in a tango, lost in the night.

Whispers of freedom, our spirits collide,
With stars as our witness, together we glide.
Each step a new promise, each turn a new chance,
In this fleeting moment, we share our dance.

Hearts beating wildly, we twirl and we dream,
Floating on melodies, lost in the stream.
Every heartbeat echoes, a rhythm we share,
Forever we're captured, dancing on air.

Entwined in Fate

In shadows we wandered, two paths intertwine,
A thread of connection, a bond so divine.
Through storms and through calm, we've weathered the
test,
With love as our compass, we find our rest.

Time dances forward, but we're never apart,
Two branches of one tree, forever in heart.
With each shared moment, our destinies blend,
Entwined in the journey, on love we depend.

The stars wrote our story, a dance of the skies,
In silence we listen, hear fate's softest sighs.
Together we'll flourish, as seasons will change,
Entwined in our fates, forever we'll range.

Beyond the Horizon

The sun kisses land, in a golden embrace,
Chasing the shadows, we quicken our pace.
With dreams as our compass, we sail through the night,
Beyond the horizon, where hope meets the light.

The waves sing a song, of places unknown,
Adventure awaits, for the brave and the lone.
With winds at our backs, and stars to our guide,
We journey together, where wonders abide.

Each dawn brings a promise, a canvas anew,
Painted with colors of every hue.
Together we'll reach, where the sky meets the sea,
Beyond the horizon, where we're meant to be.

Heartstrings in the Wind

A melody carries through whispers of air,
Each note a reminder, of moments we share.
With heartstrings entwined, we dance through the breeze,
In rhythms of laughter, our spirits find ease.

Through valleys and mountains, our echoes resound,
In harmony's embrace, true love can be found.
The wind holds our secrets, our dreams in a swirl,
Painting our stories, a canvas unfurled.

As twilight descends, and the stars softly glint,
Our hearts beat in time, a beautiful hint.
In this fleeting world, where moments are thin,
We'll follow the music, with heartstrings in the wind.

The Fireflies' Serenade

In the garden's gentle glow,
Fireflies dance, putting on a show.
Whispers of night in their flight,
Nature's dreams take off in light.

Softly they twinkle, bright and bold,
Stories of magic begin to unfold.
Chasing shadows, weaving tales,
In the silence, their song prevails.

Each flicker a note, a sweet refrain,
Echoing softly through the lane.
In twilight's hush, they play their part,
Lighting the night with a flickering heart.

As they waltz among the trees,
Carrying wishes on the breeze.
The evening wraps in a warm embrace,
While fireflies spark, illuminating space.

In the Quiet Corners

There are places where shadows dwell,
Secrets whispered, stories to tell.
In quiet corners, solace found,
Echoes of life softly surround.

The air is thick with memories,
Floating like leaves on autumn's breeze.
Time stands still, like a painting new,
Each brushstroke holds a tale or two.

Worn-out chairs, a threadbare quilt,
Layers of love slowly built.
In these spaces, hearts intertwine,
Binding the past, yours and mine.

Gentle sighs of a distant tune,
Underneath the glowing moon.
In the quiet corners, dreams ignite,
Filling the soul with beams of light.

Blossoms in the Breeze

Petals flutter like whispers of spring,
Carried on winds, a joyful fling.
Colors burst forth, a vibrant spree,
Nature's canvas, wild and free.

Sunlight dances, a golden hue,
Kissing each blossom, bright and new.
In the garden, laughter blooms,
Filling the air with sweet perfumes.

Beneath the blue, a soft embrace,
Every flower finds its place.
Linked by roots beneath the ground,
In harmony, life is found.

As the breeze sings a gentle song,
Blossoms sway, where hearts belong.
Together they whittle time with ease,
In a symphony of blossoms and breeze.

Threads of Connection

Invisible strings pull us near,
Binding hearts with love sincere.
In laughter's echo, in silence shared,
Threads of connection, gently prepared.

Each moment we weave, a tapestry bright,
A canvas of dreams, colored with light.
Through valleys of joy and mountains so steep,
Our bonds grow richer, our promises deep.

In the warmth of a hand, in whispered grace,
Time stands still, a sacred space.
Together we rise, together we fall,
Threading the needle through it all.

With every heartbeat, stories unfold,
In the fabric of life, love is rolled.
Cherishing moments, forever our quest,
In the threads of connection, we are blessed.

The Lullaby of Hearts

In twilight's soft embrace, they rest,
A melody of whispers blessed.
Each heartbeat sings a gentle tune,
Beneath the silvery crescent moon.

A tender gaze, a fleeting smile,
In shadows held for just a while.
The night air hums of dreams untold,
Wrapped in warmth, they dare be bold.

With every sigh, a promise sways,
In softest winds of love's displays.
The world around them fades away,
As stars begin to weave their play.

In silence found, their souls unite,
As starlight dances, pure and bright.
The lullaby, a soft refrain,
Of hearts entwined in joy and pain.

With whispers shared, they drift and soar,
A symphony of evermore.
In dreams they find their spirits free,
The lullaby of you and me.

A Canvas of Two

Two souls united, brush in hand,
Painting life in a vivid strand.
Each stroke reveals a hidden spark,
Creating color from the dark.

In shades of laughter, hues of peace,
Their canvas grows, their worries cease.
With every hue, a story spun,
Together shining in the sun.

Splashes of joy, a sprinkle of tears,
Every detail drawn through years.
With layers deep, they build their dream,
Reflecting love's enduring beam.

Awash in shades of dusk and dawn,
A tapestry that moves them on.
As life unfolds from a simple plan,
Their masterpiece, a lifelong span.

In every color, every line,
They find a love that's pure, divine.
Together, they will always know,
Their art of life continues to grow.

Mirrored Smiles

In moments shared, a mirrored gaze,
Reflecting joy in myriad ways.
With simple gestures that ensue,
A dance of hearts, a bond so true.

Each smile a spark, a silent vow,
In laughter's light, no need for how.
Together, they weave their gentle art,
In endless rhythms, two become one heart.

In moments brief, like fleeting light,
They find their way through day and night.
A glance, a grin, the world's embrace,
In mirrored smiles, they find their place.

As shadows stretch, and dusk draws near,
They gather close, and fate is clear.
With every smile, a story tells,
In mirrored joy, their magic dwells.

For in each smile, reflections shine,
A language shared, a love divine.
In this embrace, they find their style,
In every day, they mirror smiles.

Whispered Dreams

Beneath the stars, their secrets flow,
In whispered dreams, a soft hello.
The night unfolds in tender grace,
With every word, they find their space.

Their hopes entwined like vines that climb,
In shadows cast by passing time.
With every sigh, the whispered thread,
Weaves stories of the paths they tread.

In moonlit hues, their visions gleam,
A tapestry of every dream.
With gentle hands, they shape the night,
Creating futures, pure and bright.

With each embrace, the world feels right,
In whispered dreams, they take their flight.
Through stardust paths, they take their leap,
In silence deep, their love runs steep.

So let them drift on waves of night,
In whispered dreams, they find their light.
Together, strong against the stream,
In unity, they chase their dream.

Harmony of Spirits

In the quiet whispers of the night,
Where stars align in gentle flight,
Souls connect in a dance divine,
Breathing in the sacred sign.

With every heartbeat, rhythms blend,
A symphony that has no end,
Echoes in the space between,
Unified, a timeless scene.

Through shadows cast and light that glows,
The essence of our being flows,
Weaving tales in twilight hue,
A harmony, forever true.

In the stillness, dreams take wing,
Together, we rise and sing,
Treading paths of love and grace,
In this enchanted, sacred place.

Bound by threads unseen yet strong,
In this collective, we belong,
Through the winds and gentle tides,
Our spirits dance, our joy abides.

Radiance of Togetherness

Underneath the golden sun,
We gather, hearts as one,
With laughter that ignites the air,
In every moment, love we share.

Like flowers blooming side by side,
In this garden, we confide,
Vivacious colors, bright and bold,
Stories of our lives unfold.

Hands entwined, we face the storm,
In unity, our hearts stay warm,
Through trials, we find our light,
Guided by hope, we ignite.

With every step, a shared embrace,
In the rhythm of this space,
Together, we are intertwined,
A tapestry of love defined.

In the glow of evening's grace,
Reflecting joy, the world we trace,
In the wonders we create,
Together, we elevate.

Traces of Enchantment

In the forest, secrets lie,
Whispers of the earth and sky,
Traces left by moonlit dreams,
Dancing in ethereal beams.

Each step on the ancient ground,
Magic woven all around,
Where shadows play and laughter peals,
The heart of nature gently heals.

Through the mist, a vision glows,
Painting paths where wonder flows,
Every leaf, a tale to tell,
In this enchanted wood, we dwell.

As twilight paints the world anew,
With hints of gold and shades of blue,
We trace the dreams of old and wise,
In the glow of starry skies.

With open hearts, we roam and seek,
For magic calls to those who speak,
In the tapestry of night,
We find the whispers of delight.

Garden of Infinite Possibilities

In a garden rich and vast,
Seeds of hope are gently cast,
Every bloom, a promise bright,
Nurtured by the sun's warm light.

Dreams take root in fertile ground,
Where endless wonders can be found,
With every petal, stories grow,
In this space, we learn to flow.

Colors mingling, vibrant and free,
Each flower sings in harmony,
Expressions of the heart and soul,
A canvas where we all are whole.

Through the seasons, change unfolds,
In the stories that nature holds,
We learn to thrive in every way,
Celebrating life's grand ballet.

In this haven, dreams arise,
Beneath the vast and open skies,
Together, we cultivate our fate,
In the garden, we create.

The Garden of Us

In the garden where we meet,
Flowers bloom, our hearts skip a beat.
Sunshine dances on our skin,
Whispers shared where love begins.

Petals soft as sweetest dreams,
Beneath the sky, our laughter streams.
Colors blend, a vibrant hue,
Every shade reminds me of you.

Time stands still in nature's embrace,
Each moment shared, a sacred space.
Roots entwined, we stand so tall,
In this garden, we'll never fall.

Through gentle rains and sunny days,
We nurture love in countless ways.
Seasons change, yet still we grow,
In the garden, our love aglow.

Let the world around us fade,
In the spaces we have made.
Together here, forevermore,
In this garden, we explore.

A Season of Togetherness

As blossoms bloom, we walk as one,
Beneath the warmth of springtime sun.
Hand in hand, we greet the day,
In every moment, love's ballet.

Through summer's heat and autumn gold,
Every story shared, a tale told.
In cozy nights, we find our peace,
In each other, our joys increase.

Winter whispers through the nights,
Fires crackle, casting lights.
Together, we brave the chill,
With every heartbeat, love we feel.

In every season, side by side,
Our hearts connect, they will not hide.
Cultivating dreams, strong as trees,
In this journey, love's sweet breeze.

A tapestry of moments spun,
In every season, we have won.
Together in laughter, tears, and bliss,
A season of us, sealed with a kiss.

Starlit Soliloquy

Under the blanket of the night,
Stars above, they burn so bright.
Whispers soft as evening air,
In your gaze, I find my prayer.

Moonlight dances on your face,
In this stillness, time finds grace.
Each twinkle sings our secret song,
In this moment, we belong.

Cosmic thoughts and dreams take flight,
Speaking truth in soft moonlight.
In silence, we exchange our fears,
With starlit hopes and tender cheers.

Gravity pulls, our souls entwined,
In every chance, our hearts aligned.
Galaxies swirl in vast embrace,
In your love, I've found my place.

Under this starlit canopy,
You are the world, the heart of me.
Together, we can touch the skies,
In this soliloquy, love lies.

In Each Other's Eyes

In each other's eyes, worlds unfold,
Stories untold, secrets of old.
With just one glance, we bridge the miles,
In silence, we share countless smiles.

A universe held in a gaze,
Within this moment, love ablaze.
Every twinkle tells a tale,
In this realm, we shall not fail.

Reflections dance, a vibrant spark,
In your gaze, I find my mark.
The mirrored depths hold timeless grace,
In each other's eyes, our sacred space.

Through storms and calm, our eyes express,
Life's canvas painted, love's finesse.
In every blink, the truth we see,
In your eyes, I'm truly free.

So here we stand, hearts open wide,
In this journey, with you as my guide.
Each moment shared, a precious prize,
Forever found in each other's eyes.

Colors of the Unseen

Beneath the vibrant, hidden glow,
A silent dance of shades we know.
In twilight's grasp, they softly blend,
Where dreams and shadows twist and bend.

In whispers bright, they weave their tale,
Like distant stars that gently sail.
Each hue conceals a world untold,
A tapestry of light and gold.

Through eyes wide shut, we seek to find,
The palette rich, the ties that bind.
In every shade, a secret lies,
A spectrum born from silent sighs.

The blaze of autumn, crisp and bold,
Winter's chill in hues of cold.
Spring awakens with gentle grace,
While summer's warmth ignites the space.

In every corner, life's embrace,
The unseen colors leave their trace.
An artful dance beneath the sun,
Where every shade is never done.

Whispers in the Mirror

Reflections dance on gleaming glass,
Whispers float as moments pass.
Fragments of the soul revealed,
The truth within is gently sealed.

Each glance a secret, softly shared,
In silent spaces, hearts laid bare.
Beneath the surface, echoes blend,
A silent pact, a timeless friend.

The mirror holds what eyes can't see,
A tapestry of memory.
Within its frame, a story swells,
In whispered tones, the spirit dwells.

Time draws lines where dreams are traced,
Into the depths, our fears are faced.
Once vibrant hopes, now shadows gray,
In quiet whispers, fade away.

Yet hope persists with every glance,
In fragile light, we find our chance.
The mirror speaks in tender tones,
In every crack, the heart atones.

Echoes of the Heart

In beats that pulse through silent nights,
Echoes ring with tender lights.
A rhythm born of love's sweet strain,
In every moment, joy and pain.

Through corridors of time we roam,
The heart, a compass leading home.
In laughter's sound and sorrow's song,
Echoes remind us where we belong.

Each thump resounds like thunder's call,
Awakens dreams, both great and small.
In each refrain, the past survives,
A melody that ever thrives.

As seasons shift and years unfold,
The heart's deep tales are gently told.
In whispered sighs and shouts of glee,
The echoes linger, wild and free.

With every pulse, a story's spun,
From dusk's embrace to morning's run.
In echoes of the heart, we find,
The beating truth that leaves us blind.

Fragments of Affection

In pieces scattered, love is found,
Like autumn leaves on hallowed ground.
Each fragment holds a memory's light,
A glimpse of passion, soft and bright.

In letters written, words unsaid,
In fleeting glances, love is bred.
Tiny tokens of a shared dream,
In simple things, the heart may gleam.

From laughter shared on rainy days,
To whispered secrets in soft ways,
Each moment, precious, carefully kept,
In fragments, love has softly crept.

Through seconds, hours, days, and years,
These little snippets hold our fears.
In memories warm, or chilly strife,
The heart collects the hues of life.

In every shard, a story lies,
A testament to laughter, sighs.
In fragments small, love finds its place,
In every touch, a soft embrace.

Pages of a Shared Story

In a world made of whispers, we find our way,
Each page holds a memory, come what may.
Ink flows like rivers, carrying dreams,
In the quiet of night, our love softly gleams.

The chapters unfold, with laughter and tears,
Every line we write erases the fears.
Hearts intertwined, through thick and through thin,
In the book of our lives, together we spin.

Turning the pages, we savor the time,
With every new story, our hearts learn to rhyme.
Adventures await, on horizons so wide,
With each shared adventure, there's nothing to hide.

Through seasons of change, the ink may fade,
But the essence of us in those words will cascade.
Holding each moment, cherishing the flow,
In the pages of us, love continues to grow.

Together we journey, in the tale of our fate,
Each word stitched with meaning, it's never too late.
In the narrative of us, forever we stay,
In the pages of a shared story, come what may.

Symphony of Memories

In the silence of dusk, melodies rise,
Notes woven with laughter, beneath velvet skies.
Each sound is a whisper, a soft serenade,
A symphony of memories that never will fade.

We dance through the echoes, hearts in sync,
In the rhythm of moments, we stop and think.
Harmony's sweetness, like honey it flows,
In the symphony of memories, love ever grows.

The chorus of love calls through time's gentle hands,
Chasing the sunlight, where the music lands.
Strings of our stories, they play in the air,
In this orchestra of life, our hearts lay bare.

From crescendos of joy to soft undertones,
Each note is a treasure, each melody known.
The past intertwines with the present's embrace,
In the symphony of memories, we find our place.

As long as we gather the sounds of our days,
With the fire of love, and the warmth of its rays.
Together we'll sing, through the highs and the lows,
In this symphony of memories, our passion glows.

Portraits of Intimacy

In the gallery of hearts, we find our stance,
Captured in moments, we dance a sweet dance.
With every brush stroke, our colors collide,
In the portraits of intimacy, we take pride.

Eyes locked in silence, a story unfolds,
A canvas of trust, where love gently molds.
The whispers of secrets in soft shades align,
Creating a masterpiece, eternally divine.

Each touch is a color, vibrant and bold,
Intertwined emotions, through the warmth we hold.
In the brush of his fingers, the world disappears,
In these portraits of intimacy, there are no fears.

Layers of laughter, of passion and grace,
In art we find solace, our sacred space.
Captured in layers, the depth of our souls,
Portraits of intimacy, where love makes us whole.

As time brushes on, our frame holds the light,
Forever displaying, through day and through night.
Together we linger, as life ebbs and flows,
In the portraits of intimacy, our love only grows.

Vows in the Twilight

Underneath the canopy where stars softly gleam,
We speak of our future, our hearts intertwine seam.
In the twilight's embrace, our promises flow,
In whispered vows, the world becomes slow.

With the dusk as our witness, we pledge to be one,
Two souls in a journey, together begun.
Through storms and through sunlight, we'll share our
fight,
In the sacred silence, our love takes flight.

Each vow is a treasure, a promise so true,
In the tapestry woven, it's me and you.
Hand in hand we walk, in that soft golden light,
Making memories anew, as day turns to night.

The twilight sings softly, as shadows retreat,
Echoes of love in the gentle heartbeat.
With every soft promise, our future ignites,
In the vows of the twilight, our love shines bright.

Through seasons of time, we'll cherish this bond,
With hearts ever open, of each other, we're fond.
In the twilight we'll linger, as night falls so right,
In the vows of our love, forever, we unite.

Glimmers of Affection

In the quiet of the night,
Stars twinkle with delight.
Every moment feels so right,
Warmth envelops, love's pure light.

Soft whispers in the air,
Promises of what we share.
Your gaze holds a tender flare,
A connection beyond compare.

Through the shadows we dance,
In each other's arms, a chance.
Our laughter sways in trance,
In love's eternal expanse.

Time stands still, hearts entwined,
In your soul, my peace I find.
With every heartbeat aligned,
Together, forever combined.

Glimmers of affection shine,
In your heart, forever mine.
In this moment, we define,
A love that's truly divine.

Echoes of Heartbeats

In the silence, soft and clear,
I can feel you drawing near.
Every heartbeat, I revere,
A melody only we hear.

Whispers float like autumn leaves,
Carried by the breeze that weaves.
Inside your embrace, time deceives,
In love's comfort, my heart believes.

Your laughter rings like a chime,
Echoing through the fabric of time.
Each moment shared is so sublime,
Together, we create our rhyme.

In the twilight, stars ignite,
Guiding us in the softest light.
With you, every wrong feels right,
In the dark, you are my sight.

With every sigh, our love grows strong,
In this symphony, we belong.
Together, we face right and wrong,
Echoes of heartbeats, our song.

Shadows of Tenderness

In the dusk, shadows softly fall,
Embracing whispers, a gentle call.
In your eyes, I see it all,
Tender moments, love enthralled.

Every laugh, a treasured spark,
In your warmth, I shed the dark.
Within your touch, I feel the mark,
Of tenderness that leaves its arc.

Beneath the moon's watchful gaze,
Our hearts dance in this quiet haze.
In a world that often betrays,
Together, we find our ways.

With every beat, our spirits blend,
In this love, I find a friend.
Through thick and thin, we comprehend,
In shadows, our hearts transcend.

A safe haven, your arms provide,
In your presence, love won't hide.
Through every storm, by your side,
In shadows of tenderness, we abide.

Whispers on the Wind

Soft whispers float upon the breeze,
Carrying dreams with such ease.
In the distance, love's sweet tease,
A gentle touch that aims to please.

Each moment shared, a secret told,
In your arms, I feel so bold.
With every glance, the world unfolds,
In whispers of warmth, our love enfolds.

Through the trees, our laughter plays,
In the warmth of summer days.
With you, troubles fade away,
In whispers on the wind, we stay.

Time slips by, yet we remain,
In every joy, in every pain.
With every heartbeat, we sustain,
In love's embrace, our soul's refrain.

Let the world around us spin,
In this dance, we both shall win.
Together, we begin again,
With whispers on the wind within.

Whispers on the Breeze

The leaves dance gently in the air,
Soft secrets woven everywhere.
A melody lingers, sweet and light,
Carried softly into the night.

Stars twinkle softly in the sky,
Each one a wish that floats nearby.
Moonlight bathes the world in grace,
As shadows play with a tender face.

Footsteps wander on the earth,
Echoing stories of love and mirth.
With every sigh, a heart beats true,
In harmony with skies so blue.

The wind carries tales untold,
Of dreams and hopes, both brave and bold.
Each whisper dances from tree to tree,
A symphony of what could be.

In this hush, we find our peace,
As nature sings, our worries cease.
Embracing moments, soft as air,
Whispers woven with heartfelt care.

Portraits of Togetherness

In laughter shared, our hearts unite,
Canvas of memories, pure delight.
Colors blend in vibrant hues,
Each brushstroke tells of love infused.

Hand in hand, we face the storms,
Through trials, our bond transforms.
With every glance, a story spun,
In the tapestry of two as one.

Sunset paints the evening sky,
With whispered dreams that never die.
Together we create the frame,
A picture rich with joy and flame.

The quiet moments, soft and sweet,
Where simple joys and life both meet.
In every hug, a promise stays,
The warmth of love in countless ways.

As seasons change, we bravely stand,
In portraits drawn by a gentle hand.
With hearts as canvases, we find,
Togetherness that's rare and kind.

Ethereal Dreams

In dreams we dance on clouds of light,
Past the stars that shine so bright.
Whispers of hope fill the air,
As we dive into realms of dare.

The night unfolds its mystic cloak,
With every word, a spell is broke.
Floating high on wishes made,
In a world where fears just fade.

Time stands still in this gentle place,
Where shadows swirl in soft embrace.
A journey drawn by the heart's desire,
With every thought, our spirits fly higher.

Through corridors of endless dreams,
Life's beauty flows in endless streams.
In every sigh, new worlds ignite,
As we wander through the night.

Awake or lost in slumber's hold,
These ethereal visions never grow old.
Together we chase the light, it seems,
In the realm of our cherished dreams.

The Story We Write

With every word, our tale unfolds,
In ink of courage, the heart beholds.
Chapters crafted with love's embrace,
Each sentence filled with time and space.

We pen our sorrows, joys, and fears,
With laughter echoing through the years.
Each moment captured, raw and true,
The narrative shaped by me and you.

In twilight's glow, the pages turn,
Where lessons learned allow us to yearn.
As dreams intertwine with reality's thread,
The story stretches, never dead.

Together we weave our history's thread,
In colors that dance, and words unsaid.
A tapestry bright, a journey so wide,
In the story we write, we abide.

Through trials faced and mountains climbed,
The essence of us is perfectly rhymed.
In every ending, a new start ignites,
This is the magic of the story we write.

Kaleidoscope of Yearning

In colors bright, hearts intertwine,
Each shade a tale, a love divine.
Through whispered dreams and silent sighs,
We chase the stars that light our skies.

Fragments of hope in patterns swirl,
Each twist and turn a dance, a whorl.
In the tapestry of night we sail,
With fervent wishes on the gale.

Chasing shadows, we long and yearn,
For each reflection, a lesson learned.
In moments fleeting, we find our way,
Embracing the colors of the day.

Through swirling storms, our hearts remain,
Bound by the threads of joy and pain.
In every hue, a piece of soul,
A kaleidoscope that makes us whole.

So let us weave our dreams tonight,
In vibrant shades, a pure delight.
With every heartbeat, we create,
A world where love can captivate.

Songs of Serenity

Soft whispers dance through twilight haze,
As nature hums her gentle praise.
With every breeze, a tranquil tune,
That lulls the heart beneath the moon.

In quiet corners, shadows play,
Embracing dusk in sweet ballet.
The world stands still; the heart takes flight,
In harmony that feels just right.

Each note a feather, light and free,
Floating on waves of memory.
The stars reply with twinkling eyes,
A serenade beneath the skies.

With every breath, the night unfolds,
Its secrets whispered, gently told.
In the calm embrace of midnight's grace,
We find ourselves in solace's place.

So let us sway to nature's song,
In this stillness where we belong.
Together wrapped in peace so rare,
We find our joy within the air.

Timeless Bond

In the stillness of the night,
Two souls converge, a sacred light.
Through laughter shared and silent tears,
We craft a bond that spans the years.

No distance can our hearts divide,
In every heartbeat, love's sweet guide.
As seasons change and moments pass,
We cherish memories like glass.

With gentle whispers in the dark,
Our spirits light a lasting spark.
In every glance, a story told,
A treasure greater than pure gold.

Through trials faced, we stand as one,
In life's embrace, we've just begun.
A timeless bond that will not break,
In every choice, in every mistake.

So here we stand, with hearts entwined,
In every moment, love defined.
With each new dawn, our truth aligns,
In the tapestry of hearts, it shines.

Sentiments in the Moonlight

Beneath the moon's soft, silver glow,
Our spirits dance and freely flow.
In whispered dreams and quiet sighs,
We find the truth that never lies.

With every heartbeat, secrets shared,
In the stillness, love declared.
The world fades softly into night,
In shadows deep, our hearts take flight.

We speak in starlight, bright and clear,
In quiet moments, hearts draw near.
Each glance a promise softly made,
In moonlit paths where dreams cascade.

So let our souls in silence twine,
With every breath, a love entwined.
In the hush of night, let passions churn,
For every touch, our hearts discern.

In the twilight hour, wrapped in bliss,
We find ourselves in every kiss.
Together woven, light and dark,
In the moon's embrace, our love's sweet spark.

Captured in Time

Moments flicker like a flame,
Echoes of laughter, whispers of names.
Time weaves tales, both old and new,
Captured in memories, like morning dew.

Fleeting seconds dance and play,
Chasing shadows as night meets day.
A photograph lost in a gentle breeze,
Frozen in time, a heart's sweet tease.

Worn pages of dreams left untold,
Secret stories in chambers of gold.
With every tick, a journey unfolds,
Captured in time, a treasure to hold.

Whispers of yesteryear softly sigh,
Reminiscing moments that never die.
Painting the future with strokes of the past,
Captured in time, a spell that will last.

In the silence, a heartbeat speaks,
Fleeting glances and soft, warm cheeks.
Every memory, a thread finely spun,
Captured in time, we're never undone.

A Riddle of Hearts

Two souls wander, paths intertwine,
In the garden of love, they softly shine.
Eyes mirror secrets, unspoken delight,
A riddle of hearts, under stars so bright.

Words like petals, gentle and soft,
Each syllable lifting, like dreams aloft.
With every glance, a puzzle unfolds,
A riddle of hearts, a story retold.

Laughter dances on the edge of night,
An echoing promise, future so bright.
Threads of connection, woven with care,
A riddle of hearts, forever to share.

In silence they sit, knowing so well,
The verses of love, a sweet, timeless spell.
Fingers entwined, whispers take flight,
A riddle of hearts, in the soft moonlight.

With every heartbeat, mysteries grow,
In the hush of the night, their love's gentle flow.
Two destined paths, not lost, but near,
A riddle of hearts, forever sincere.

Shadows in the Light

Beneath the sun, where shadows dance,
Light weaves stories, whispering chance.
Every flicker, a life newly born,
Shadows in the light, where dreams adorn.

The sun dips low, a golden embrace,
Casting warmth on a familiar place.
In the twilight hues, lovers unite,
Shadows in the light, their spirits take flight.

Silent echoes of moments gone past,
In the balance of day, memories cast.
The gentle sway of leaves in the breeze,
Shadows in the light, bringing hearts to ease.

Through the branches, the sun's rays gleam,
Illuminating hopes, igniting a dream.
In the quiet, soft whispers ignite,
Shadows in the light, an endless delight.

Every heartbeat a shadow, every smile a beam,
Together they paint a beautiful theme.
In the dance of the dusk, love finds its might,
Shadows in the light, eternally bright.

In the Arms of Serenity

Where the rivers flow and the willows weep,
In the arms of serenity, our souls gently sleep.
A hush in the air, the world fades away,
Wrapped in stillness, come what may.

Moments of quiet, where thoughts can roam,
Finding solace in nature, a comforting home.
Whispers of peace in the rustling leaves,
In the arms of serenity, the heart believes.

Stars twinkle softly, like dreams taking flight,
Guiding lost hearts through the tranquil night.
Every breath, a promise, sweet and alive,
In the arms of serenity, we learn to thrive.

Mountains stand tall, guardians of grace,
Cascading rivers leave a gentle trace.
In this essence, our spirits ignite,
In the arms of serenity, everything feels right.

Through life's raging storms, we find our way,
In quiet acceptance, we learn to sway.
Embraced by the calm, our fears take flight,
In the arms of serenity, life feels so right.